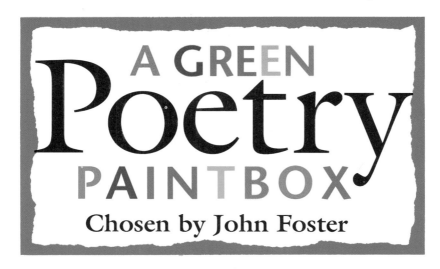

A GREEN Poetry PAINTBOX

Chosen by John Foster

Oxford University Press

Oxford University Press, Walton Street, Oxford OX2 6DP

Oxford New York Toronto
Delhi Bombay Calcutta Madras Karachi
Kuala Lumpur Singapore Hong Kong Tokyo
Nairobi Dar es Salaam Cape Town
Melbourne Auckland Madrid

and associated companies in
Berlin Ibadan

© Oxford University Press 1994

Oxford is a trade mark of Oxford University Press

First published in paperback 1994
First published in hardback 1994

A CIP catalogue record for this book is available
from the British Library

Illustrations by

Jane Bottomley, Caroline Crossland, Paul Dowling, Fiona Dunbar,
Jane Gedye, David Holmes, Rhian Nest James, Anita Jeram,
Ann Johns, Thelma Lambert, Jan Lewis, Bethan Matthews,
Diana Mayo, Jan Nesbitt, Zoe Pearson, Valeria Petrone,
Claire Pound, Steve Rigby, Graham Round, Chris Smedley,
Andrew Tewson, Martin Ursell, Marc Vyvian-Jones, Jenny Williams.

ISBN 0 19 916678 1 (paperback)
ISBN 0 19 916719 2 (hardback)

Printed in Hong Kong

Contents

Eggs

Each day I crack my breakfast egg
I hope more and more
That one day when I crack it
Out will pop a dinosaur.

Celia Warren

I'm a Diplodocus

Hocus, pocus,
plodding through the swamp;
I'm a Diplodocus,
chomp, chomp, chomp!

Grass for breakfast,
I could eat a tree!
Grass for lunch and dinner
and grass for tea.

I'm a Diplodocus
plodding through the swamp,
hocus, rocus, pocus,
chomp, chomp, chomp!

Judith Nicholls

6

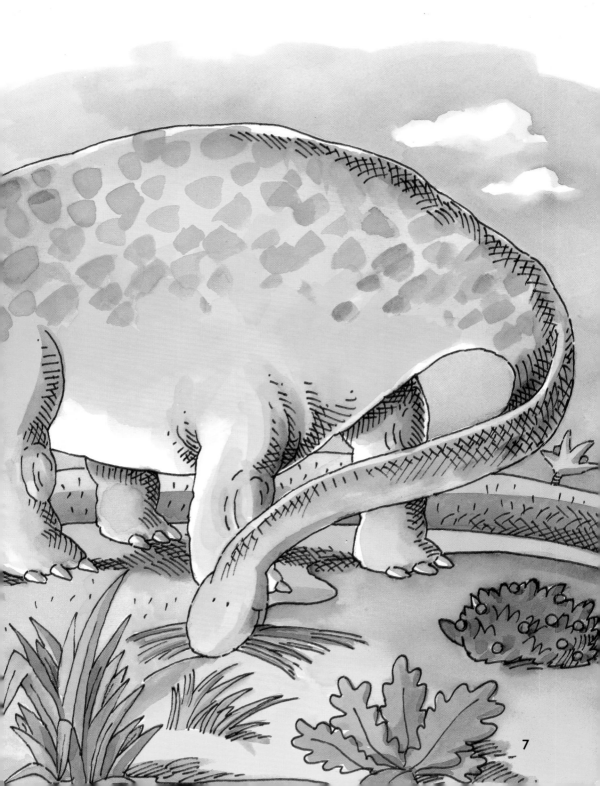

That's what you think!

I made a model dinosaur.
'My name's T. Rex,' it said.
I ran to tell our teacher.
She laughed and shook her head.

'You must have been day-dreaming.
Models can't talk,' she said.
'That's what you think!' growled a voice.
Our teacher screamed and fled!

Doreen Dean

CLASS MARKS - 35

Dream pet

I dreamed I owned a dinosaur,
I kept it as a pet,
He really caused a panic
When I took him to the vet.

I shoved him in the waiting room,
A woman gave a shout,
The dogs all started barking,
So I had to take him out.

The dinosaur was so afraid
He hid behind a car.
The vet said 'You're too big to hide,
I know just where you are!'

Before the vet could calm him down
He'd galloped to the park,
His big teeth made a racket
As they chattered in the dark!

Sue Benwell

Dinosaur dreams

Dinah Shore
dreamed she saw a dinosaur
knock on her window with its claw.

Dinah Shore
dreamed she saw a dinosaur
peeping round her bedroom door.

Dinah Shore
dreamed she saw a dinosaur
sleeping on the kitchen floor.

Dinah Shore
dreamed she saw a dinosaur
wake up and give a mighty ROAR!

John Foster

It's raining out

'It's raining out,' said Mum to me,
'So don't forget your hat.
You're going to need your wellies, too.
You can't go out like that.'

I put my hat and wellies on
And went out in the rain.
I ran through puddles big and small
That I found down in the lane.

I went and shook the holly bush.
It dripped all over me.
I chased a frog down by the pond,
Then I went home for tea.

'Just look at you,' said Mum to me,
'You've ruined your nice new hat,
And got your wellies soaking wet.
You can't come in like that!'

David Andrews

The Great Water Giant

The Great Water Giant
has finished his bath.

He pulls the huge plug
out of the clouds.
He roars his thunderous laugh
and a wet, slippery waterfall
spills out of a squelchy sky.

'Look out below,' he seems to shout,
as the water

```
s         p         g
p         l         u
l    s    i    p    s    s
o    p    s    l    h    l
o    l    h    o    e    u
s    a    e    s    s    s
h    s    s    h         h
e    h         e         e
s    e         s         s
     s
```

and soaks deep into the thirsty earth.

Ian Souter

The day the hose flipped

'Right,' said Dad,
'I'll turn the hose on
Round the back.'
We were washing the car—
It was really black.

We waited a bit
Me and our Chris,
Then the water came through
With a noisy hiss.

The water came through
With a splutter and a gush,
It came bursting through
With a mighty rush.

And the hose came alive
Like a twisting snake.
It soaked Chris's jeans
As if he'd jumped in the lake.

19

It drenched my dress.
The hose still flipped about,
And next door's cat
Got a waterspout.

When Dad arrived back,
He said, 'Gosh!
It's *the car* that's supposed
To be getting a wash!'

Eric Finney

21

The sea

The sea can be angry.
The sea can be rough.
The sea can be wild.
The sea can be tough.

The sea can rip.
The sea can tear.
The sea can roar
Like a hungry bear.

The sea can be gentle.
The sea can be flat.
The sea can be calm
As a sleeping cat.

The sea can glide
Over the sand,
Stroking the beach
Like a giant hand.

John Foster

The wuzzy wasps of Wasperton

The wuzzy wasps of Wasperton
Are buzzing round the plums
And sucking all the juicy ones
Before somebody comes.

The wuzzy wasps of Wasperton
Are buzzing round the pears
And choosing all the ripest ones—
They think the orchard's theirs.

The wuzzy wasps of Wasperton
Steal fruit fit for a king.
But don't disturb them if you go—
Those wuzzy wasps can STING!

Daphne Lister

Ants

Dad says I've got ants in my pants
when I can't sit still at all,
but the only ants I ever see
are crawling on our garden wall.

Brian Moses

Spider in the bath

I've picked up frogs,
And patted dogs,
Stroked the skin of snakes.
I've tickled cats,
Examined bats,
Fed the ducks and drakes.

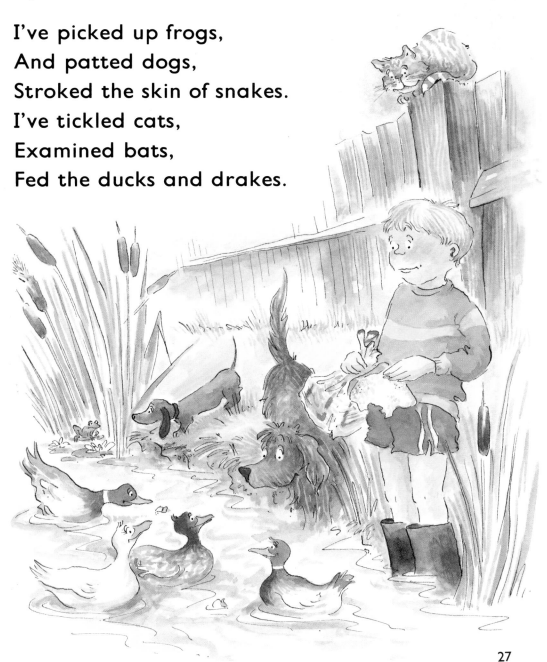

I've chased fat hens,
Pushed sheep in pens,
Held chickens in my hand.
Been stung by bees
On both my knees,
Pulled crabs out of the sand.

I've watched a mole
Go down his hole,
Followed ants along a path.
So why am I
So frightened of
A spider in the bath?

Lynette Craig

A bluebottle is

A bluebottle is
a buzz,
a whizz!
He's faster than you,
a dazzle of blue,
that's what he is!

A bluebottle is
a buzz,
a whizz,
a dive,
a zoom,
a catch-if-you-can,
a rocket for one,
THAT'S what he is!

Judith Nicholls

Stick insect

Pick an insect,
stick an insect
on the kitchen floor.
Which is insect,
which is twig?
Who knows any more!

Judith Nicholls

Water boatman

Across the pond
the boatman rows.
Where he came from
nobody knows.

He dips and dives
from space to space.
The pond is still,
he loves to race!

What can he see
as he darts by?
Below, dark weeds.
Above, blue sky.

Across the pond
the boatman rows.
Where is he going?
Nobody knows!

Judith Nicholls

33

My den

With a cardboard crate
and an empty sack,
a broken buggy
and a plastic mac,

down in my garden
under the tree,
I've built a home
and it's just for me.

Tony Mitton

Castle

I wish I lived in a castle
with flags and pointed towers.
I'd stand up high on the battlements
and look at the land for hours.

And if I spotted a dragon
or a giant, looking bored,
I'd strap on all my armour
and chase it away with my sword.

Tony Mitton

High and dry

In swampy places
homes are found
that stand on stilts
above the ground.
The wooden stilts
are sunk in mud
to keep the homes
above the flood.

Tony Mitton

Empty cottage

Down at the end
of the country lane,
there's an empty cottage
with cracked window panes.

The door's off its hinges.
The roof tiles leak.
The only sounds
are a rustle and creak.

Only the spider,
the slug and the louse
live in the shell
of the old empty house.

Tony Mitton

I need a gas mask

When I walk around town,
it's really busy
and the smell of car fumes
makes me dizzy.

When I go in the café
for a drink and a cake,
the cigarette smoke
makes my head ache.

When I sit on the bank,
where the river flows,
the smell is so bad
that I hold my nose.

When I stand near the factory
and the wind's from the south,
it stings my eyes
and blows grit in my mouth.

With all these horrible
things in the air,
I need a gas mask
to go anywhere.

Charles Thomson

The bird on the shore

*A sticky skin of oil
is floating on the sea
and any bird caught in it
needs our help to break free.*

Just like the gull we found,
half-dead among the sands.
We wrapped him in a towel
but still he pecked Dad's hands.

'It's not a job for us,' Dad said,
'He needs some expert care.
I think I know a place.
They'll make him better there.'

They scrubbed and cleaned our gull,
then showed us several more,
which had been black with oil
and half-dead on the shore.

A sticky skin of oil
is floating on the sea
and any bird caught in it
needs our help to break free.

Brian Moses

We've got to start recycling

Take all your old glass bottles
To the bottle bank in town,
So they can use the glass again
By melting it all down.

Don't dump your old newspapers
With the rubbish in the tip.
Save them all, then put them
In the green recycling skip.

Don't throw away your drink cans,
Their metal's useful too.
We've got to start recycling.
It's up to me and you!

John Foster

Grandad says

On the pavements, in the streets,
Bags from crisps, wrappers from sweets.
Rubbish rots in roads and gutters.
'What a mess!' Grandad mutters.
'Keep things tidy, keep things clean.
Make the world fit to be seen.'

Irene Yates

Out in all weathers

It snowed in the night
And the whole world is white.
I'm off out with my friends
For a mighty snow fight.

It's windy today
And the trees swing and sway;
See the wind take my kite
Up, up, up and away.

Today it's all rain—
It's really a pain.
I could just stay in
And watch telly again.
But maybe not yet:
Instead I'll just get
My wellies and things—
And go out and get wet.

Eric Finney

Snow

Soft snow has fallen
During the night,
The grass snuggles under
A carpet of white.

We climb in our wellies
Then button up warm,
Make footsteps in circles
Around the white lawn.

We roll up the snow,
Make snow-bricks to stack
And build a white giant,
A snowman called Jack.

When I look through my window
Much later at night,
Jack is just standing
Silent and white.

Jack Ousbey

Weather at work

I'm a speeding hailstone,
An icy lump.

I'm a clap of thunder,
A noisy thump.

I'm a chilly snowflake,
soft and white.

I'm a ray of sunshine,
warm and bright.

I'm a falling raindrop,
sploshing to the ground.

I'm a winter snowball,
hard and round.

I'm a flash of lightning,
A magic sight.

You can see me zigzag,
Lighting up the night.

Jenny Morris

Lost and found

'If you're lost,' said Mum,
'What you must do
Is ask the police
And they'll help you.'

Last night, we were walking
Through the fun fair.
When I looked round
Mum and Dad weren't there.

So I asked a policewoman
What I should do
And she said, 'Don't worry,
I'll find them for you.'

As we walked along,
She held my hand.
Then we went in a van
By the hot-dog stand.

She told me to sit
And wait in a chair,
Then suddenly
Mum and Dad were there!

So if you get lost,
What you must do
Is ask the police
And they'll help you.

John Foster

Emergencies

Red alert!
Red alert!
I've dropped my lolly
in the dirt.

SOS
SOS
I've spilt some custard
down my dress.

999
999
I've ridden my bike
through the washing-line.

Ambulance,
and make it quick!
I think I'm going
to be sick.

Tony Mitton

Tree emergency

Emergency! Emergency!
Our Jamie's gone and
Got stuck up a tree.
We lifted him up
To get the ball,
Now we've got that back
But he can't move at all.
Get on the phone quick,
Emergency!
Fire, Police, Ambulance—
We'll need all three.

How high up is he?
Well, not very high.
We could reach him
From the garden chair.
Why don't we try?
Rescue party quick!
I'll show you how.
He might have got down
On his own by now.

Eric Finney

Lifeboat rescue

The waves are huge.
There's a howling gale.
The tiny boat
Has lost its sail.

The coastguard
Spots the tiny boat,
Sees a girl struggling
To keep it afloat.

He sounds the alarm.
Emergency!
The lifeboat sets off
Across the sea.

The huge waves try
To block its way.
But the lifeboat hurries
Across the bay.

The girl is rescued,
And once again
A life is saved
By the lifeboatmen.

John Foster

Many ways to travel

There are many ways to travel
and one that I like
is to zoom down a hill
on a mountain bike.

There are many ways to travel
and another that's nice
is to slide on a sledge
on the snow and ice.

There are many ways to travel
and isn't it fun
to sail on the sea
in the wind and sun?

There are many ways to travel
but the best by far
is to ride on a rocket
to a distant star.

Tony Mitton

Mr Mad's machine

Mr Mad has made a machine
To take you round the world.
Its wheels are square. Its tail is long.
Its wings are thin and curled.

It blows out rings of purple smoke.
The engine squeaks and squeals.
The jets are very powerful.
They're made of cotton reels.

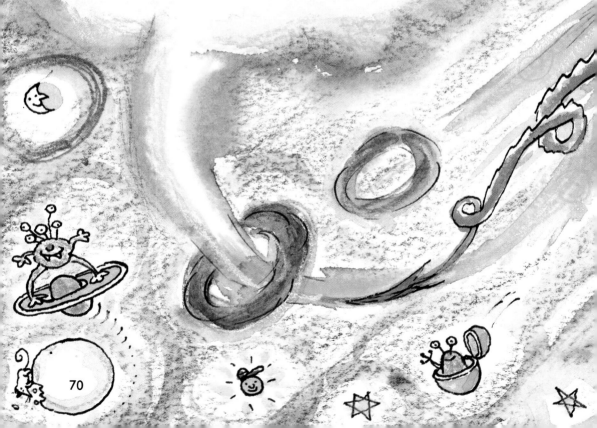

I wonder what it would be like
To fly in the machine.
It is the strangest sort of plane
That I have ever seen!

Tony Mitton

71

The Skateboard Twins

Here she comes,
Sally Green!
We all call her
the Skateboard Queen.

WHOOSH!

And here comes Sammy,
her best mate.
Sammy is a champ
on the kingsize-skate.

They swerve and they spin.
They never trip.
Sally does a twist
with a backward flip.

Sammy does a spinner
round the bins.
Sally and Sammy
are the Skateboard Twins!

Tony Mitton

Night ride

When I can't sleep
I shut my door
And sit on the rug
On my bedroom floor.

I open the window.
I close my eyes
And say magic words
Till my carpet flies.

Zooming over gardens,
Chasing after bats,
Hooting like an owl
And frightening the cats.

Then when I feel sleepy
And dreams are in my head,
I fly back through my window
And snuggle down in bed.

Celia Warren

75

The flood

When Paula left the tap on,
She flooded the whole school.
The classroom was a lake.
The hall was a swimming-pool!

Gopal floated paper boats.
Joanna splashed about.
The head was in a temper.
You should have heard her shout!

I had a water fight
With Mary, James and Paul.
That's why we spend our playtimes
Sitting in the hall.

Charles Thomson and John Foster

Travelling to school

If the playground was a runway,
I would fly to school by plane.

If the staff room was a station,
I would steam to school by train.

If the classroom was a stable,
I would ride in at a trot.

If the main hall was a harbour,
I would sail to school by yacht.

But it's just an old brick building
With an iron gate,
And if I don't start running,
I'm going to be late.

John Coldwell

All in a day

I tried hard
to keep my socks clean,
but aren't PUDDLES fun!

I tried hard
to keep my shirt clean,
but aren't PAINTS fun!

I tried hard
to keep my trousers clean,
but isn't MUD fun!

I tried hard
to keep my sweater clean,
but aren't PLAYGROUNDS fun!

I tried hard
to keep MYSELF clean,
but Mum,
isn't *SCHOOL fun!*

Judith Nicholls

In our classroom

In our classroom
There are
Brown eyes, blue eyes,
Grey eyes and green.
Brown hair, black hair,
Yellow hair and green.
Brown hands, pink hands,
Grubby hands and green—
Green eyes,
Green hair,
Green hands—
Don't stare—
It's a visitor from space!

Irene Yates

Visiting Grandma

Benjamin is jumping.
Benjamin is glad.
He's going to visit Grandma
With his sister and his dad.

They're going to Jamaica.
They're flying in a plane.
They're going for a fortnight,
Then they'll fly home again.

Benjamin is smiling
For his holiday's begun.
He'll soon be in Jamaica
With his grandma in the sun.

Celia Warren

Drinks

Mum likes tea
From our big blue pot,
Kept under the tea cosy
Very hot.
Dad likes coffee
In his large brown mug:
What a lovely smell
As it steams in the jug!

Gran likes cocoa:
A nice hot cup
At any time of day
Makes her eyes light up.
And when Mum's and Dad's
And Gran's drinks are made,
I pour myself
Ice-cold lemonade.

Eric Finney

Second best

I never get anything new.
With three older brothers,
My clothes come from others.
Does this ever happen to you?

Ian Larmont

When Grandad took me to the zoo

When Grandad took me to the zoo,
Grandma said,
'You make sure he behaves himself.'
But he didn't.

He made faces at the monkeys,
he poked a penguin with his stick.
He went far too close to the tigers
and he woke up an angry snake.

He called the hippos names,
he dropped ice-cream down his shirt.
He queued to go on the slide
till a zookeeper sent him out.

Then as we left he said,
'We'll come back as soon as we can.'
'Sorry Grandad,' I answered,
'Next time I'm coming with Gran!'

Brian Moses

Index of first lines

Acknowledgements

The Editor and Publisher are grateful for permission to include the following poems:

David Andrews for 'It's raining out' © 1988 David Andrews; Sue Benwell for 'Dream pet' © 1993 Sue Benwell; John Coldwell for 'Travelling to School' © 1993 John Coldwell; Lynette Craig for 'Spider in the bath' © 1993 Lynette Craig; Doreen Dean for 'That's what you think' © 1993 Doreen Dean; Eric Finney for 'Drinks', 'Out in all weathers', 'The day the hose flipped' and 'Tree emergency' all © 1993 Eric Finney; John Foster for 'Dinosaur dreams', 'Lost and found', 'Lifeboat rescue', 'The sea', 'We've got to start recycling' all © 1993 John Foster; Ian Larmont for 'Second best' © 1993 Ian Larmont; Daphne Lister for 'The wuzzy wasps of Wasperton' from BBC Poetry Corner © 1989 Daphne Lister; Tony Mitton for 'Castle', 'My den', 'High and dry', 'Empty cottage', 'Emergencies', 'The Skateboard Twins', 'Many ways to travel' and 'Mr Mad's machine' all © 1993 Tony Mitton; Jenny Morris for 'Weather at work' © 1993 Jenny Morris; Brian Moses for 'Ants', 'The bird on the shore' and 'When Grandad took me to the zoo' all © 1993 Brian Moses; Judith Nicholls for 'I'm a diplodocus' © 1988 Judith Nicholls, previously published in 'Popcorn pie' (Mary Glasgow Publications), for 'Stick insect' © Judith Nicholls, previously published in 'Higgledy-humbug' (Mary Glasgow Publications), and for 'A bluebottle is', 'Water boatman', 'All in a day' and 'Tyrannosaurus Rex' all © 1993 Judith Nicholls; Jack Ousbey for 'Snow' © 1993 Jack Ousbey; Ian Souter for 'The Great Water Giant' © 1993 Ian Souter; Charles Thomson and John Foster for 'The flood' © 1993 Charles Thomson; Charles Thomson for 'I need a gas mask' © 1993 Charles Thomson; Celia Warren for 'Eggs', 'Night ride' and 'Visiting Grandma' all © 1993 Celia Warren; Irene Yates for 'Grandad says' and 'In our classroom' both © 1993 Irene Yates.